Great Project Management

A Quick Guide

Jon Calpin

Table of Contents

Introduction

You've got your PRINCE2 accreditation, you've followed that up with an Agile course, and maybe you've even hit the heights of getting your Managing Successful Programmes (MSP) qualification. Great. You now have all the tools you need to be a great project manager.

Except it doesn't really feel like it, does it? What these courses, and many more like them, will give you is a process and a framework for managing projects and programmes. They can tell you which documents to produce at what stage and how you move from one project phase to another, and so on. And this is important; you need this. But what they aren't designed to do is equip you with the soft skills you need to deliver projects successfully.

How can you stop suppliers walking all over you, for example? How do you get the best out of your team? How do you really run a planning session? How can you get better at reporting? This guide is an attempt to address such issues which I don't think are taught enough at a practical level, often leaving new project managers with the extremely daunting task of learning on the job.

I've tried to pick out the issues that I think really get to the core of the job. My own field is national IT projects, and the examples I give in this book do relate to this. However, I've tried to steer clear of the more technical aspects, and hope you'll be able to take away plenty from here whichever sector you work in.

You might also notice that I've used the terms 'projects' and 'programmes' slightly interchangeably. I probably could have written a whole chapter on the differences between projects and programmes. Ultimately, though, the skills required for both are virtually the same.

I can't guarantee that this book will turn you into a great project (or programme) manager, but whether you're new to projects or an old hand, I hope you find something here to make you a better one.

This might seem too obvious a point to start with, but it's the fundamental question: what problem are we trying to solve? And how are we going about trying to solve it? If this can't be answered and easily explained in layman's terms to just about anyone, then you'll have problems. It'll be difficult to engage with stakeholders and suppliers, and senior management won't properly buy in. Worse still, different groups of people, including within the project team, will have a different take on what the project is. This is a surprisingly common problem, and the longer the confusion drifts the more difficult it is to get everyone on the same page.

Many years ago, I joined a project that had been underway for several months. It had a lot of smart people on the team, all real experts in their field. Not one of them could explain what the fundamental purpose of the project was. They were working hard, solving problems – but to what end? The senior management had long given up asking, and many of the team were completely demotivated.

So clarifying the project's purpose really is the first task you need to get on top of. Later, I'll cover the detailed planning elements, documenting what's in and out of scope, and how to get that approved. But for now, this is about you as project manager (PM) developing a high-level understanding, and making sure all the various interested parties agree (or at least identifying where and why they don't).

Obviously, a lot of this will depend on the stage at which you join a project. For the purpose of this section, we'll assume you're joining somewhere near the beginning. By the time a PM has been appointed, there's usually something in train even it's just a couple of people in the organisation who've identified a business driver and most likely a subject matter expert (SME). So there's probably some structure to things, an idea of what the project should be, and the bones of a project team.

Give yourself a few of weeks to get to grips with what the project's about and don't worry too much at this point about documentation and formal controls. There's often a temptation to immediately prove you're adding value by churning out plans – but try and resist this. It might go against the grain a little but if you can just focus on your own understanding at this point, you'll take the immediate pressure off and give yourself time to really get under the skin of things.

These are the sort of questions you need to be posing to yourself and others:

- *Why has the business commissioned this? (Or why is the business considering commissioning this?)*
- *Who in the business has commissioned this?*
- *What's the business's current landscape?*
- *What will be different about the business after the project is delivered?*

- *Were other options considered? Have they been definitively ruled out?*
- *Has it been decided who's delivering the capability? Internal or external teams?*
- *How much senior management buy-in is there?*
- *What governance is in place?*
- *Who are the obvious stakeholders? What's their view on the project fundamentals?*
- *Who are the less obvious stakeholders? What do they think?*
- *Who are the users?*
- *What's actually been agreed so far?*
- *What's the budget approval situation?*

Tip: Even if you're joining the team when the project's further down the line, it's still worth stepping back and trying to answer these kinds of questions. Although things should be more set-in stone by this point, it's your job to challenge and it's possible that many questions remain unanswered.

There's no shortcut to this task. You need to speak to a lot of people, and you need to make a lot of notes. You'll have to speak to many of them quite a few times as you check your understanding and clarify why people are telling you contradictory things.

So be pushy. Ask the dumb questions early (they won't be dumb). And be confident. You're smart – you can understand this stuff. So what if you ask the same question a couple of times? It shows you really want to understand and get to grips with things.

Most importantly, cast your net wide. What do other interested parties think your project's purpose is? Do they agree with it? If not, why not? This is a great chance for early stakeholder engagement and gaining wider buy-in. At this point you aren't just telling them what you're doing (or what you think you're doing), you're asking them what they think you should be doing. People like to have their opinion listened to, so keep an open mind.

As well as grappling with the project fundamentals, this is also a good opportunity to start understanding your team. Who's being defensive? Who doesn't seem to agree with the project's goals (if it has any yet)? Who might even be lying to you?! Don't make any value judgements on these people yet. Wait until you've got the full picture – including the history of how this is the twentieth time the organisation has attempted this and why it'll definitely fail this time too. (I guarantee someone will say this to you almost word for word.)

You should be spending most of this period listening rather than speaking. There's a real tendency, particularly I think in IT projects, to prove you understand everything immediately, or even that you already know about xyz. But this doesn't show strength or depth of knowledge and can actually come across as a bit insecure. Worse than that, you aren't creating an environment where you can have meaningful conversations to learn more about things.

The team will respect you for a listening approach, and many of them might well be in the same boat as you at this point.

* * *

Ok, so you've spent a couple of weeks or so digging into what you're supposed to be doing and why. You've established yourself as a credible person who's keen to understand the project and listen to different viewpoints. And you're now at a point where you can spend 10–15 minutes talking knowledgeably about it.

You now need to speak to your senior management team to relay your findings. Do they agree? Are they on the same page? Where are the gaps? This isn't just about demonstrating how clever you are at picking it all up; you also need to outline what happens next. Which is that you're going to write it all up.

The level of detail in what you write will depend on what point you're at in the proceedings. If you're about to start a small discovery piece, then there's no point in producing a 20-page document with a 200-row project plan. You just need a light document explaining your approach, resources, timescales, costs, the likely direction of travel and what your final outputs will be.

If you know where the project's going and things are reasonably well defined, you can produce a more substantial project initiation document (PID) or similar.

This will go into far more detail and include risks and issues, plans, etc.

Tip: You should still go through this exercise even if you join a project when it's further along. You need to review the existing documentation against your findings. Do they align? Is it still describing the project you're delivering?

When producing these documents, keep in mind that people who have very little knowledge of the detail need to find them readable. I've read too many that have a bewildering amount of detail without really addressing that fundamental question: what problem are we trying to solve and how? I think this stems from a lack of understanding of why these documents are produced, or sometimes from an organisation's overly rigid, formulaic approach to them, using templates with lots of mandatory sections to fill in regardless of their relevance to the specific project.

The purpose of these documents is to give the people commissioning the project enough information to decide whether to go ahead or not. As PM it's your job to ensure you're giving them that information. A narrative needs to flow through the document: you're telling a story about what you're going to do and why.

Don't try and overly 'sell' the project at this point. Even if you're certain that commissioning it will alter the course of human evolution, try and keep it understated and calmly lay out the potential benefits against the risks and issues (we'll get into those later). There's a time and a place for a sales pitch and this isn't it.

So that's the happy path if you like. But let's just focus for a minute on that person who will inevitably think this project is all a waste of time. Certainly, some people seem to take a real pleasure in sniping and doing things down, and such negativity can be really draining. But what if they're right? What if this project is based on assumptions that don't match reality? What if another project is already up and running which will either clash with or obviate the need for this one?

You can't ignore this. Obviously, you can't just take one person's word for it, but you do need to explore these issues and test them out with other stakeholders. Is there something in it? If not, then you can explain to them why they're wrong ... They won't suddenly turn into a cheerleader for the project but at least you've taken time to look at their concerns.

If they're right though ... well, you need to escalate this quickly. This is best done informally at first. Talk it through with your boss. Maybe there's some other information not widely known and that's why this project makes great sense. But in my experience, it's often the case that the naysayer has been naysaying for so long that senior management have just stopped taking them seriously.

If you've identified a compelling reason that the project shouldn't go ahead, then good for you for joining the dots.

Tip: Never assume some grand strategic plan and tactical brilliance at the level above you. People are making decisions with limited information and with their own biases. It's entirely reasonable and, in fact, necessary to challenge the project fundamentals.

At whatever point you join a project as PM, there'll almost certainly still be key questions that can't be answered. A key skill is learning to live with an element of ambiguity.

I once worked on a huge government procurement project. We needed to centrally procure a suite of products to provide a national email system for the NHS. I was quite junior on the team and the problem, as I saw it, was that we weren't really sure what that suite of products should be. Worse still, I was the only person on the team who seemed particularly bothered by this.

We had a hugely experienced team of email, procurement and commercial experts. So what was I missing? Well, we didn't know exactly what we needed because it was too early to know. There were still questions to answer. What could the market offer? What did the NHS really need? What was the best value for money? It was only relatively late on in the project that we could really state our exact requirements – which was fine.

So, learn to live with some ambiguity; don't be driven mad by it. You can't know everything at the outset and even if you could, the landscape – from business drivers to project sponsors – might change.

It's Friday afternoon. You're frazzled. You've hardly made any progress this week for reasons mostly beyond your control. And now it's one hour before your weekly report deadline. Half of the team still haven't sent you their reports so you're flying half blind, and the report template is full of sections that aren't relevant to your project which drives you mad. Worse still, you've been in exactly this position every single Friday afternoon for your entire career ...

There's always going to be some element of weekly and/or monthly reporting that you have to do. That's a given. It's completely reasonable that your organisation expects this from you, and you should have a similar expectation that your team report to you.

I'll share a few specific tips on how to make this process easier and more productive but, first, we need to fundamentally change the way we view the task of reporting. We need to stop thinking about it as a bureaucratic pain in the neck and start seeing it as a good way to take stock of the week's progress, to interact with and support your team, and to communicate genuine messages to your management. But how?

Firstly, if you need to get a report in on Friday and rely on other people's reports to feed that, then those reports need to be with you by close of play on Thursday.

Secondly, block out time in your diary on Friday to compile the report. Give yourself the whole morning if required – this isn't a job you should be rushing. Giving yourself enough time to do tasks properly is the easiest way to make them less stressful.

Most importantly, though, coach your team so that they clearly understand what information you require from them. Otherwise, at least one person in your team will submit a really shoddy report that's just a re-tread of the week before (and they'll even have forgotten to delete some of the now out-of-date information), while someone else will inevitably irritate you by giving you chapter and verse on the most trivial elements. The first person probably thinks you don't really care in any case and suspects you don't read them. The second isn't sure what you want so gives you literally everything. The point is if you don't tell them, they can't magically know what you need. So explain what level you want and why, and share your own report as a good example. This is the nuts and bolts of management, and you should feel confident in having these conversations.

Take time to read and digest the reports that are coming to you. Don't just scan through them and copy and paste the juicy bits into your own report. You should be having one-to-ones with your team every week, so use the reports they've sent you to drive those conversations (and schedule them as part of your now blocked-out Friday morning). You should find that you're better able to get under the skin of all the report content. Perhaps that person who's going into so much detail on a seemingly trivial element is on to something; you might have underestimated its importance. Also, they'll tell you things that they'd never write down … You'll find out, for example, that the innocuous-sounding line in their report, 'Finance are struggling to schedule a meeting slot,' actually means, 'Finance are no longer speaking to us as they've heard we're about to have our funding pulled and so they don't think there's any point'. And then in your own report that week, this might become, 'We need to give Finance more confidence in the long-term funding viability of this project'.

Or maybe you don't include that last line in your report. You're the PM. You're a problem solver and you've got the budget. You talk to Finance yourself and explain to them there's an approved budget for this project. Don't fall into the trap of just being a conduit for flowing information. Some things you'll need to escalate; some things you'll need to sort out yourself.

So perhaps that line in your report actually becomes: 'Not progressed as well as we'd have hoped with Finance. There still seems to be some confusion on budgets. I've scheduled in a meeting next week with the finance director to go through this'. Or if your boss wasn't really expecting any progress, then don't include it at all.

I promise your team will like this approach (although maybe not at first). They certainly can't complain anymore that the report's pointless as it doesn't get read anyway. And this will drive up the quality.

Tips: For reports coming to you, it's up to you what template to use. Keep it simple with just a few headings along the lines of: progress this week, plans for next week, and milestone dates with any slippage and reasons.

If you want the reports in by close of play on Thursday, then make sure that's understood and that this doesn't mean 10am on Friday. If people are on leave on Thursday, then you need their report by close of play on Wednesday.

If you're on leave yourself, you need to nominate someone else to write your report. I'd suggest the person who's usually late with theirs – see how much they like hassling people on a Friday. Realistically, though, you need to rotate who you nominate or it will look like you're playing favourites.

***

So you now have a crack team who have fully embraced a new, positive outlook on reporting. But it's still Friday and you still haven't written your own report …

Time to swap places with your team and think about what you want your boss to know and what you might need some help with. You want to demonstrate progress, obviously – but be honest about problems you're having. The worst thing you can do is present a relentlessly upbeat version of events, as a) no one will believe it, and b) they'll be completely blind-sided when problems come to light at a point when it's serious.

As in the above example regarding Finance, if you've identified a problem, explain it candidly and say what you're doing to sort it out. If you do need to escalate something that's beyond you to fix, state it clearly and suggest a course of action: 'I think we may need senior input with the finance director as we're struggling to get any engagement'. You will probably need to follow this up: you can't assume they'll pick it up from the report (they might not have read this book). That's easy, though – you just say: 'You may have picked up from the weekly report that I think you need to speak to the finance director'. They can't say they haven't, of course, but they'll be grateful you've given them a nudge.

So be factual, transparent, dispassionate, candid, concise. Be honest. Be political.

Lastly, even if you know your report isn't getting read properly, or is just going to a central report repository and you'll never get a single word of feedback, still do a professional job on it. Yes, maybe you could get away with copying and pasting from your team reports and dashing something off in 10 minutes. But that's not you, is it?

'Ok, there has to be some reporting up, but do I really have to spend hours every month prepping for the project board? And then writing it all up? They never read the minutes anyway.'

'We go to all this effort but the project board is just a glorified team meeting.'

'Every agenda item is just me presenting to the board … I'm just a punchbag for them.'

'They don't offer any help or support; they just criticise …'

'Every risk and issue has got my name against it … How can this be?'

'Half of them don't turn up regularly for the board, and I'm not sure the half that do turn up really understand what we're doing.'

'What difference would it really make if we just stopped having a programme board?'

'I think the chair hates me …'

'The chair definitely hates me …'

'They all hate me …'

'I'm having to spend two hours every month re-writing the minutes … Why can't the minute taker do their job properly?'

You've said at least three of the above, haven't you? I've said all of them many times …

So, firstly, what do we really mean by project or programme governance?

There could well be a complex structure of project and programme boards that you must negotiate. But whether it's a project board or a programme board, whether it's monthly or every two to three months, this is an important event for you. It's your chance to showcase the project to senior stakeholders, to escalate problems, and to potentially get decisions made. But, most importantly, it's your chance to give the board members confidence that the project is being well run.

You MUST take this seriously and do a good job.

Before addressing how, it's worth just stepping back and looking at what we really mean when we're talking about a project board.

Here's the definition from PRINCE2:

> *The Project Board has the following duties: **To be accountable for the success or failure of the project**. To provide unified direction to the project*

and Project Manager. To provide the resources and authorize the funds for the project. To provide visible and sustained support for the Project Manager.

It adds:

It's made up of the customer (or executive), someone representing the user side and someone representing the supplier or specialist input.

The Project Manager reports regularly to the project board. The board is informed of progress and any foreseeable problems.

The project board provides the Project Manager with a set of necessary decisions. They determine how the project will proceed and overcome its problems.

The Managing Successful Programmes (MSP) approach to programme boards is similar but it more tightly defines the chair as the senior responsible owner (SRO), i.e. the person from the business who is ultimately responsible for the delivery of the programme.

For the purposes of this section I'll refer to the project board.

Depending on the organisation and the stage you've joined the project, there may already be a project board up and running with an agreed membership and approved terms of reference.

However, if it's still early stages, or the project just doesn't have a board, then it's a good opportunity for you to a) suggest/initiate one, and b) shape it both in terms of attendees and direction.

Assuming the latter, you'll need some variation on the following attendees:

Chair. Ideally this needs to someone from the business side of things (the sponsor in PRINCE2 terms) rather than project delivery. It mustn't just be your boss. This person needs to be invested in, and responsible for, the delivery of the project.

A senior user. Again, this needs to be someone from the business who has a stake in the outcome of the project. So, for example, if you're running a project to build and roll out call-centre software, this person might be the head of Customer Care.

A senior supplier. This really depends on the nature of the project but usually there's an external supplier involved in delivering the solution. If the solution is being developed in-house, however, then this person might be the head of the development team.

There are generally other interested parties on the board too. I've worked a lot in the NHS and normally there'd be some clinical representation. It's wise to have someone from Finance on board (assuming they've eventually got back to you). Obviously, every project is different so we can't be too prescriptive here but there should be about six or seven attendees, including you.

Something you need to watch out for is attendees losing interest after a couple of board meetings People like the idea of being on the board, but that can soon wane and then there's a danger of it becoming just another standing meeting that people drift in and out of. The move to working remotely with endless Teams/Zoom calls has exacerbated this problem. But if the right people aren't at your board, you'll have put in a lot of effort for just three people, you won't be able to get decisions made and the whole thing will lose credibility. Your project will then suffer as a result.

So make sure you've got the right people with a stake in the project to begin with. If it does just become a team meeting with a couple of externals, this needs addressing as it won't be giving you what you need. Make sure it's a face-to-face meeting as this will give it gravitas. Most importantly, make sure it's a professional, productive meeting that people see the value of and want to attend (more on this later).

If there isn't already a terms of reference document, you'll need to create one. Don't go overboard with this; you just need to outline the board's responsibilities. It's likely to be along the lines of:

- *Ensure the project delivers on its objectives.*
- *Approve changes to the scope of the project.*

- *Approve finance and timelines, including any changes to them.*
- *Takes decisions as required during the project's term.*

Obviously, that's quite broad – and deliberately so.

List the attendees, and how often they need to meet. Include a standing agenda:

- *Introductions and apologies*
- *Review and approval of the minutes and actions from the previous board*
- *Project update (you to do)*
- *Risk and issues (you to do)*
- *Finance update (Finance to do but you'll probably end up doing)*
- *Any other business.*

That gives you the bare bones and then you can add agenda items to this as required.

You also need to include that the project team will take responsibility for: scheduling the board; sending out the board's papers (one week in advance); taking the minutes and sending them out (one week post meeting); knowing who's attending each board and who's sent apologies; and chasing actions.

Just a note on minute taking. You can't present updates, lead discussions *and* take the minutes, so you will need a good project support person to do the latter. The minutes will go out in your name, so you'll need to sign them off before they're circulated for board approval. This is always a bit fraught until the person taking the minutes has got into the groove of how you want them done. Still, try and take a few notes yourself if possible and be clear about actions – spell them out during the meeting. You can also really help out the minute taker by pausing the flow of the conversation and re-iterating what's just been discussed. The chair should do this but don't be afraid to jump in yourself.

Tip: Never ever say during the meeting, 'This bit isn't for minuting.' It doesn't sound knowing and edgy; it just sounds like you've watched too much low-quality TV.

So expect to do a bit of re-writing at first but do it in a collegial way and don't get snotty with the project support person – they aren't a mind reader. As a rule, keep the minutes brief and ensure the actions are held in a separate log which states who is assigned to each task (they'll nearly all be assigned to you).

Even if the board and its members are already up and running when you join the project, do be prepared to make suggestions that can get it closer to the model outlined here. We'll look at managing up later on.

That was a bit of a trawl through the housekeeping side of things. But if you can get that right, then that's half the battle.

So how do you get the board working for you and the project?

Firstly, you need to accept that this is on you as PM. You're managing the project, so you know best the state of play, what needs bringing to the board, the status of the risks and issues, and so on. This means you get to set the agenda.

We've already established a standing agenda and it may be that sometimes that's as much as you need. Don't try and crowbar items in just because it feels a bit light on occasion. Discuss it with the team as well: is there anything they think you should be taking to the board? And make sure you ok the agenda with the chair beforehand. Although you're driving this, you don't want to be overt about it.

Your general project update needs to be issued as a paper with the board pack. It needs to be formal but punchy. And when you're delivering it at the board it's fine to go a bit off-piste and spell out what's between the lines. Expect some challenge here and make sure you're properly prepared on the issues. If there's a particularly technical element which you know you're going to struggle with, take the technical person along to help you field questions. It's a team effort after all. (Actually, it would be a good idea to have the tech person on the board.)

Risks and issues should all be included in the board pack, but don't go through them all at the board. Just go through the major ones and any that you think the board can help with or should at least be aware of.

In terms of additional agenda items, don't come at this from the angle of: 'We've got a board next week – what can we take to it?' It should be the other way round: 'We've got these issues – we need to raise them with the board'.

When you've identified a particular issue, you need to present and explain it clearly in a paper and suggest options for dealing with it, spelling out exactly what decision you need the board to make. Most importantly, you need to know which way you want that decision to go.

An example is probably the best way to illustrate how to play this.

I was programme manager on a large-scale two-year NHS digital programme to introduce a new coding system in primary care. This impacted every single patient record in GP systems across England, and we had four GP system suppliers to help deliver the changes.

We had a great team and good relationships with the suppliers. However, it became apparent that the suppliers just couldn't hit our original timescales. Not great, but not entirely unexpected either. So we broke it down, worked out what we could live without in the first tranche of deliverables, and the suppliers committed to the remainder within a given timescale. There would be a bit of an overrun on the project, but we could absorb that in savings we'd identified elsewhere. We had a plan.

So we now needed to take this plan to the project board for agreement and approval. That should be easy then: write up a board paper outlining the problem, offer a couple of options including the above, and recommend that as our preferred one. The board would consider the paper, discuss, and approve. All good? No, all wrong.

In fact, there's a good chance that this approach would have played out in the following way instead ...

Although the board paper would have gone out a week beforehand, no one would have read it until the day of the board, and probably not until you were presenting it at the meeting itself. Not being close to the detail, they wouldn't really be able to assess the impact of the delay, however soothing the tone of your paper. All they'd hear is 'supplier delay' ... and that you seemed to be ok with it. One or two of them would suggest this was unacceptable, and others might then join in. No one would be listening, and the nuance of the solution would be completely lost. 'Why are you letting the suppliers run rings round you? You do realise this is taxpayers' money?' It would now be a feeding frenzy and there'd be nothing you could do to defend yourself without making it sound worse.

Even if it didn't descend into blood sport, you wouldn't get the decision you were after. It's human nature not to like being put on the spot to make decisions, particularly if it's one you'd rather not be faced with. Forget that the board would have had the paper for a week and could have got in touch with you to discuss it. That's not the way of the world.

So you need to get the board on side individually. Give them all a call and talk it through. Explain why you're doing this so they aren't blindsided at the board. They'll appreciate you taking the time. They won't feel a need to grandstand, and they'll probably agree with your plan. Even if they don't, at least you'll know why beforehand, and then you can bring them into the conversation at the board: 'Xxx, I know you have some specific issues with the paper ...' You're in control this way and you're far more likely to get the decision you need.

There is an element of theatre about a board, and that's ok. As the above example demonstrates, boards aren't necessarily the best forum to arrive at informed decisions. So lay the groundwork beforehand. You particularly need to ensure the chair is informed of anything major before the board. You'll be putting them in an uncomfortable position if they're only hearing about a serious setback, or indeed a win, at the same time as the other board members.

I really can't overemphasise the extent to which your credibility hinges on how you conduct yourself here. It doesn't matter how well the project is being run and how well it's delivering against its objectives – if you aren't coming across as a confident, competent person who's completely on top of the project, then you're sunk. So spend time on it. Practise your delivery if you need to.

Once people have lost confidence in you, it's very difficult to get it back. Conversely, even if things aren't going very well but you're doing a professional job at the board, people will be less concerned.

'... There are known knowns; there are things we know we know. We also know there are known unknowns; that is to say we know there are some things we do not know. But there are also unknown unknowns – the ones we don't know we don't know.'

Donald Rumsfeld, February 2002

'Everyone has a plan until they get punched in the mouth.'

Mike Tyson, August 1987

So, firstly, what do we mean by planning? Put simply, it's what we need to build, do and deliver to achieve our project outcomes. It's working out how long each aspect will take, the order they need doing in, how much they'll cost, and who's going to do them.

Planning is difficult. You've got limited and sometimes contradictory information to work with. Your senior team want to know, not unreasonably, exactly how much the whole thing is going to cost and how long it will take. The people you need to help work this out are reluctant to be forthcoming as they don't want to be held to dates and costs. And as well as this, there's a whole raft of external dependencies which could blow things off course.

It's highly unlikely you'll ever start any project with a blank piece of paper. The fact that someone's even thinking about commissioning a project means some thought will have gone into the general shape of it. For our purposes, let's assume that your organisation thinks there's some merit in standing up a project team to introduce a new customer service system.

Now, in days gone by, this would have immediately led to a team being set up with an emphasis on software delivery. You'd probably have a team of business analysts who'd start working with the business to document requirements. The developers would dive into a technical solution, and then a bit further down the line, some thought would be given to how to roll it out to users. You can probably see the flaws in this immediately. The project would be too tightly defined at the beginning, and locked into an early technical solution. Only when it was rolled out would a lot of the problems come to light.

There's a long roll call of projects that have failed after following this course. The public sector rightly gets a lot of criticism for these often high-profile failures, though in fairness the private sector has been equally guilty.

From a planning point of view, the PM would have lost control of such a plan quite quickly. They would have tried to answer the 'How long is a piece of string?' question when perhaps the question should have been, 'How strong does the rope need to be?' By the time it came to rolling out the system, the plan would have become almost meaningless as crisis management kicked in.

So a much more common approach for organisations nowadays is to commission an initial discovery phase. This short phase with just a small team is about stepping back and looking in the round at the problem that needs to be solved and the options for solving it. It's as close to the 'blank piece of paper' scenario as you're ever likely to get, and it's a great chance as PM to really get under the skin of things and plot a course forward.

The first thing you need to do in a discovery phase is pull together a list of problem statements that are owned and approved by the business. To do this you will need to talk to the business — hopefully that's obvious but it's worth saying because people who work in IT do tend to just talk to other people who work in IT, and that approach always fails.

So in our customer service system example, you and the business analyst (or similar) need to speak to the call centre managers and senior customer care managers, as well as to departments who use customer service data downstream, such as Marketing and Credit Control. And, of course, you'll need to speak to the users (you'll get a lot from talking to users).

At the end of this task, you should have a short list of problem statements along the following lines:

1. *There are currently three different IT systems being accessed by the call centre teams to meet customer queries. This is causing delays in*

customer interactions, meaning the teams'
service level agreement (SLA) targets are
consistently being missed. Currently, only 25% of
calls are below the SLA target time.

2. *Due to the data being stored across three*
   different platforms, substantial operational effort
   is required to migrate the data to a central data
   warehouse for use by teams such as Sales &
   Marketing. This requires two full-time data
   analysts at a cost to the organisation of £x per
   annum.

3. *The business is incurring significant operational*
   and licensing costs to maintain four systems
   (including the data warehouse). These are
   approx. £x per annum.

4. *Two out of the three call centre systems have*
   been designed and built using now-redundant
   technology. The input screens are difficult to
   navigate and contain many bugs which the call
   centre staff must work around. Again, this is
   contributing to SLA targets being missed.

Hopefully you've noticed that we linked the problems to a business outcome and haven't just left them open-ended.

Now you need to agree these problem statements with the project sponsor. The last thing you want is to present your findings at the end of the discovery phase only to find out that they thought you were looking at a cyber security issue.

Tip: Some of this may seem obvious, but blindly assuming everyone is on the same page is where so many projects go wrong. People are busy, they're dealing with a lot of different projects and have a really limited knowledge of your area. If you've done much public speaking, you'll know that you're supposed to speak slightly more slowly than might seem natural. Similarly, with projects you need to spell things out more clearly than might seem necessary, as what's obvious to you isn't necessarily obvious to everyone else.

Once the problem statements are agreed, your task then is to identify some high-level options for dealing with them. You need to work with the business's technical teams and commercial teams to produce this.

You aren't looking for a fully planned and costed project at this point, but each option will need an idea of the costs and time required to deliver, and any other pros and cons. You need to give the sponsors enough information to make an informed decision.

For our call centre project, the recommendations may be along the lines of:

- *Option 1: Do nothing. Accept the situation and costs as is.*

- *Option 2: Procure a new customer relationship management system and migrate existing systems data to it.*

- *Option 3: Carry out improvements to the most modern of the existing systems and migrate data from the other two systems.*

For each option include discussion points, such as how long will it take to procure a new solution? Does what's on the current market fit the bill? How much are the licences and service costs likely to be? How long is any migration likely to take? Do the skills exist in-house for making improvements? What are the benefits and cost savings of each option?

Hopefully the best option will recommend itself in terms of costs and benefits. If it's really close, then don't include a recommended option.

You'll need to write this up in a report and convene a meeting of the decision makers. Have a slide-pack version of the report ready to drive the meeting, and make sure you schedule enough time to have a proper involved discussion about your findings. Also ensure you demonstrate the process you went through, who you engaged with, etc, to give them confidence that you've done a thorough job. Have the team there to help you field questions. Expect challenge.

Tip: Remember that people don't like being put on the spot to make decisions in meetings. Try and talk to the attendees individually beforehand.

So, hopefully, by the end of the discovery phase you'll have an agreed way forward for the project. Not only that but you'll have things on an even keel as you will have engaged widely with the business and looked at the different options. It may seem slightly indulgent to spend a couple of months 'in discovery' but if done properly it can save a lot of pain further down the line.

One last point on discovery. There will only be a small team of probably three or four people working on this. The outputs by their nature will be high level. So I'm afraid you've got no excuse for not knowing all the detail. You need to really immerse yourself in this phase and have a complete understanding of the different options and the logic you've used to arrive at a recommendation. This won't be so true in later project stages, but it is here.

**

Let's assume then that a discovery phase has been completed either by you or someone else. There's an agreed route forward, funds allocated, and at least an idea of the timeframe and the resources required. We now must think about what products we need to produce, and what processes we need to complete, in order to achieve our aim.

I'm going to assume at this point that there are the bones of a project team in place, perhaps based on the discovery team. I've worked in this industry for over 25 years and never once have I come in as a PM with literally no one else in post. So for our purposes we'll assume we have a technical architect, a business analyst or two, maybe a junior PM, a project support office, and some commercial resource.

Where do we start then? Well, first of all, forget about project plans for the time being. We've got fundamental questions to answer before we can get to that point.

The best place to start is a workshop that gets the project team together for a whole day (off site if possible). You can badge this as a planning meeting, but really it's the project team kick-off meeting. This is a great chance to get everyone on the same page in terms of the project goals. It's up to you to lead the workshop, but you want the team to come up with ideas.

Start by articulating what success looks like. Going back to our call centre example, let's assume a decision has been made to go with the second option – procuring a new customer relationship management system, and migrating existing systems data to it. What does success in this scenario look like? A few thoughts could be:

- *A fit-for-purpose customer care system which offers improved functionality to the current system.*
- *Improved information for sales and marketing teams from the new system.*

- *A seamless migration from the four existing systems to the new system, with no data loss or system downtime.*
- *A robust ongoing service-management model.*

Even just from this limited list we can start to flesh out our products and processes.

We need to look at what's currently on the market, and let the market know we're doing this. So straightaway we can see we need a market engagement approach. Who's going to do that? Commercial? Maybe. Do they have someone who can do that? If not, do we need to bring someone in? Is that a full-time position? Doesn't sound like it, but maybe.

What is the current baseline functionality? What does the business need over and above this? We need to get business analysts on the case. Is one enough or do we need two or three? What's our approach for capturing and documenting the requirements? Once we have them, how are we going to use them as part of the procurement process?

We need a migration approach. That means we'll need the technical architect, who'll understand how the data is stored now. This probably needs to link into that market engagement piece. Which of our potential suppliers have done something similar before on this scale? They'll need access to the technical architect, who'll need access to the technical teams. Sounds like we might need a second technical architect?

What about ongoing service management? Where does that need to fit into our organisation's wider service management, if at all? Why is there no one from service management at this workshop? (They never answer the phone ...)

What's our procurement approach? We absolutely need to document that – it's a legal requirement. Have we got an idea of what that looks like? Enough commercial resources?

Do we have all our stakeholders identified? How are we communicating with them?

We're not trying to answer all the questions here; we're just working out exactly what questions need to be answered. Already you can see how we're identifying cross-dependencies, our known unknowns, and hopefully finding out about some unknown unknowns.

At this point it's also worth starting to think about what we won't be doing, i.e. what's out of scope. This can come over as a bit negative or perhaps even a bit jobsworth. However, it's important to explicitly state this and ensure everyone is on the same page from the beginning. Of course it's open to challenge, and things that are initially out of scope might well come in as the project progresses and more information comes to light. You might firmly clarify that your project won't include the procuring of a new accounts system, for example, but if market engagement reveals that many of the systems offer suitable accounts modules, then perhaps it goes back in scope. That's a decision to be made downstream.

You'll see I've used the word 'approach' quite a bit. I've worked on many projects that have produced grand strategy documents for supplier engagement and technical direction, etc, and the overriding common theme was that they were long out of date almost as soon as they were published and didn't really ever get read. Better to produce a set of punchy approach documents that set out in simple terms what each of the areas (which will become workstreams) are trying to achieve and how.

At the workshop, you want a commitment from each of the 'leads' (as they become apparent) to produce an approach document. Each one needs to set out objectives, how they'll be achieved, and what resources are required, etc. In doing this you're giving them autonomy, although obviously you will need to add input and challenge where necessary. These approach documents will be your first set of deliverables, which you should take to the project board for approval.

Once you've got the approaches identified, you'll need to drill down further and start establishing exactly what tasks and products are needed. Again, this is a team effort, best done in a workshop environment. You may be able to make a start on this at the initial workshop, but don't shy away from scheduling as many as you need. At this stage, it's more important to get it right than get it done quickly.

Tip: You're actually better having a series of shorter workshops than trying to get everything done in one long session. People's attention starts to wander after a few hours, and you won't get the input you're after.

You should be aiming to put together a list of products, who's responsible for them, who's actually producing them, how long they'll take to produce, what order they need to happen in and the planning assumptions made behind them.

You'll never be in a position where you have all the information you need to produce a perfect plan, so stating your planning assumptions is really important. The planning assumption for our call centre might initially be along the lines of:

- *Commercial resource is immediately available.*
- *The business requirements can be met by products currently on the market.*
- *The business can provide resources to support the requirements-gathering phase.*
- *The budget is approved to allow the recruitment of additional business analysts.*

One or more of these assumptions may turn out to be invalid, thus impacting the initial plan, and can be challenged when you present it.

This is a good point to start thinking about risks and issues, which we'll cover later in more detail. What's going to stop you delivering your products? Lack of resource? Lack of information? Lack of direction? You may only be able to state these at a high level at this point but do still capture them. You can flesh them out and build in mitigation plans as you progress. In terms of identifying them, some will be obvious and naturally drop out of the conversations you're having. But it's a good idea when you're looking at the success criteria in these initial workshops to also start thinking about what failure looks like. Not just abject failure in that nothing gets delivered, but partial failures too.

So as well as the seamless migration, etc, identified above, we might have:

- *Migration operation requires too much business downtime, which impacts customer service for unacceptable time frame.*
- *Manual workarounds required post migration due to system incompatibilities.*
- *Users unhappy with new input screens.*

***

We're now getting to the point where we can start to contemplate an actual project plan.

My best ever plan was in MS Project: it had nearly 400 rows (tasks), resources against each one, links between each row which denoted dependencies, and a complicated formula for working out the critical path. If one thing slipped it would immediately output a new end date for the project. I spent most of my time chasing people for progress so I could update the plan. I had the whole thing printed out on one wall of the office. I even took a version of it to a project review at the Treasury, where I spent an hour explaining it all to a panel of bemused civil servants. It ended up managing me and did nothing to help move the project forward.

So not that.

Aim for something with around 20–30 rows at most. It should have a timeline along the bottom with your major milestones mapped to it, demonstrating which order they need to happen in. Have one plan but split it into swim lanes for each workstream. Use one colour across all the swim lanes for your critical path. It's probably also worth having an executive summary of the timeline with perhaps just 10 or so rows for the project board. Getting the granularity of the information you're sharing right is important as you don't want to overwhelm people with too much. The board will just need the major milestones, for example.

It's a good idea to use this plan to drive team meetings, as long as it doesn't just become a row-by-row trawl through it. Plans are a great engagement tool: they allow different workstreams to get a view of each other and for everyone to get an all-round view of the project.

This is a good point to come back to methodology. PRINCE2 states that a project initiation document (PID) should be produced at this early stage of the project, and that it needs to contain the project aims, timescales, references to the approach documents, risks and issues, the planned budget, team make-up and size, and assumptions. This needs to be approved by the project board.

So the 'plan' should really mean the PID, of which the timeline is one element. Incidentally, the PID should be updated throughout the lifetime of the project as new information comes to light and things change. No one ever does this but it's actually a good way to keep track of when and why the project changes in direction or scope. If a project is going to run over several years, inevitably the personnel will change, and people just forget why we were going to do X but now are going to do Y. An up-to-date PID with a change control section will provide this background information.

You're going to be spending a lot of time reporting on the plan. Is it still on track? If not, why not? When will it be back on track? And so on. You need to do this with complete honesty and transparency. Don't pretend things are progressing well when you know there are problems coming down the line or already here. It might get you through a meeting, but it won't get you through the one after. No one expects everything to progress smoothly without a hitch. So be honest about delays and what they will do to overall delivery dates, and explain what you're doing to mitigate the problems (as well as what help you need to mitigate them). Explain why those initial assumptions turned out to be invalid and give the basis for new ones.

Flag problems early. If they don't materialise, then great. Never blindside anyone with bad news. If supplier engagement is going a bit cold, tell people, even if it's just informally. Then when the supplier pulls up the drawbridge it's less of a bombshell.

One of the best tools you've got to help you with all this is a decent process for risk and issues management, and this needs a whole chapter of its own.

Once you've worked out, at least at a high level, your deliverables and timeline, take a step back from it and think in the round about what you're delivering. Think about your key stakeholders and the business's priorities. Is there any way you can shuffle things and deliver an element sooner than the plan states (even if it might mean the overall timeline gets stretched a bit)? This is about identifying a 'quick win'. Perhaps the call centre network is running slowly due to capacity issues, for example. This will probably need dealing with before we migrate to the new system, so might it be worth fixing that issue now and making life a bit better for the call centre teams in the short term? Ok, but then that might need some rework when we migrate to the new system, so that does introduce a risk there. You get the idea. If your project can deliver some early value to the business, you'll be the toast of your project board and beyond.

You've got a project board next week, so you'd better look at your risks and issues log. It's the first time you've looked at it since the last board and they weren't great then … Where's the link for the log? You always have to ask the PMO for it and they're on leave. Who else might have it? Ok, you've found the link and you're in. No one's updated the ones they're responsible for, so now you're going to have to chase for updates — oh and half of the relevant people are on leave too (you need a better leave rota). Is that one really a risk or is it an issue now? Quite a lot of them don't really seem that relevant anymore; they've been overtaken by events. How can you explain that in the update? Should you just close that one off your own bat? Update them all the best you can? You probably won't get to the risks and issues at the board anyway … What you really need to do is have a proper risks and issues workshop with the whole team, and baseline all of them. Yes, you'll definitely do that … starting next month.

This is classic behaviour. It's led, quite rightly, to me having a strip torn off when the chair of a board decided he did want to go over the risks and issues, and the whole shabbiness of the log was exposed.

There are countless books and courses on how to manage risks and issues, and there are software packages to help you document and track them. There's even an institute you can join. But none of this will help you if your attitude is that this is an admin burden on a level with your monthly finance meeting (that shouldn't be an admin burden either, but you get the point). You need to have risks and issues front and centre. If you get this right, it can be a great tool for helping you manage the project. I'm going to outline a few ideas to help you. However, the most important thing is your attitude: you need to stop seeing risks and issues management as one big hassle.

In the planning chapter, we looked at some ways of identifying potential problems as part of the initial planning workshops. As these meetings progress you should be able to build up the level of detail. This has to be a team effort, both in terms of identifying these issues and working out how to mitigate them. The problem here is that nothing seems to turn people off more than being asked to attend a risks and issues workshop. So in order to ensure you're made aware of possible problems, I'd suggest discussing risk and issues as part of your team meetings when you review the plan.

Identifying possible problems, at either a high or detailed level, is one thing, but let's look at some basics for managing them.

A risk is a problem that might happen: *'There is a risk that no current commercially available products can meet our business requirement'*.

An issue is a problem that's already happening: *'We currently do not have enough business analysts to adequately capture the business requirements'*.

A risk can turn into an issue, but that doesn't mean all issues started life as risks (no one's that ahead of the game).

As well as stating what the risk/issue is, you need to spell out what the downstream implications are:

'There is a risk that no current commercially available products can meet our business requirement. This may require a change to the project scope which will increase the project timescales and budget.'

'We have an issue in that we currently do not have enough business analysts to adequately capture the business requirements. This will delay market engagement and, potentially, downstream procurement activity as we can't fully state what functionality is required.'

Ok, fine. So what are you going to do about it? You need a mitigation plan. This doesn't need to be too detail heavy – just spell out the steps.

So first the risk. You might end up having to create an internal development team to build a system that can meet your needs. Or you might need to engage a software house to build it. Or you might work with a supplier to create additional functionality. But that's getting too many steps ahead. You need to get to the facts. You need to prioritise the market engagement.

So your mitigation needs to be along the lines of:

1. *Identify commercial resource to establish market engagement approach, and execute.*

As the resource comes on board, you then add to this.

1. *Identify commercial resource. Completed 23/04/22*
2. *Produce market engagement approach. Planned 20/05/22*
3. *Supplier workshops scheduled. Planned 21/06/22*
4. *Report on viability of commercially available solutions. Planned 30/07/22*

Two points here:

Firstly, isn't this just an overview of the market engagement workstream? We'll be reporting on that in more detail in a workstream update anyway, so isn't this just duplicating effort? Partly. However, the risks will be read by far more people than the workstream update, and this is so fundamental to the project it's worth this minimal amount of effort to drive the point home with your senior management.

Secondly, this four-point plan is all very step by step. It's not all that savvy, is it? It's going to take months to find out what's currently available. Living with some ambiguity is one thing, but this?

Why not add in a step that might help?

1. *Identify commercial resource. Completed 23/04/22*
2. *Reach out to suppliers already working in this area for informal demos/discussions on their product suite. Ongoing activity.*
3. *Produce market engagement approach. Planned 20/05/22*
4. *Supplier workshops scheduled. Planned 21/06/22*
5. *Report on viability of commercially available solutions. Planned 30/07/22*

But now we've got another issue: the lack of business analysts. So we don't really know what our requirements are. Our risk mitigation plan has a dependency on our issue mitigation plan …

So what's our issue mitigation plan?

1. *Recruit additional business analysts to existing team. Progress against plan:*
   Advert gone out 01/04/22
   Interviews planned 23/04/22
   Planned start date 01/06/22
2. *Produce requirements report 1/11/22*

The dates don't work, do they? Your project's falling apart, and it's only just started.

So you need a smarter plan. But that's fine, you're a PM and a problem solver by nature. Let's take a step back. How detailed do the requirements really need to be for you to carry out some market engagement? How different are your requirements likely to be compared with other business doing similar?

Maybe the plan needs to be:

1. *Recruit additional business analysts to existing team. Planned start date 01/06/22*
2. *Using existing BA resource, document high-level business requirements for initial market engagement. Planned date 01/05/22*
3. *Produce detailed requirements report 1/12/22 (This date's slipped a month as the existing BA has had to prioritise the high-level requirements).*

These are all simplistic examples and I'm sure you can pick holes in them. But I'm trying to demonstrate how managing your risks and issues properly can really help you identify what the actual problems are, find cross-dependencies and hopefully come up with imaginative solutions.

In terms of how and where they should be documented, less is more in my opinion. The more complicated the documenting and tracking, the more unwieldy it can become. As long as there's a process and a central repository, an excel spreadsheet can do the job.

Who does the updates? This is a PM job. Your team of Python developers are never going to meaningfully update risk and issues. Accept that fact. Far better that you hold the reins and do the updates yourself for all the reasons above. Certainly you'll need to get updates from the team, but you should be doing that anyway.

In terms of reporting to the project board, take the whole log but just update them on the risks and issues that are of particular interest, or that the board can help you with, or that you think can now be closed.

You do need to be able to grade your risks and issues, from those with the potential to completely upend your project to those much further down the scale. The usual way of doing this is to look at the probability of x happening and multiplying that by the scale of the problem it will cause.

So back to our business analyst issue. Well, it's already an issue, so it's 5/5 in terms of it occurring. And its impact initially looked quite serious, so let's say the scale of the problem was 4/5. So that's a grade of 20 out of a possible 25. Now we've mitigated it, it's still an issue and we're still short of BAs, but its impact is probably now only 2/5, giving a grade of 10 overall. The issue's not to be ignored but it needn't give you sleepless nights.

Risks and issues need managing proactively with the support of your team. If you're doing it properly it can really help. Then, eventually, filling in the risks and issues log the week before the project board becomes the easy bit.

'So exactly why are we doing this?'

We discussed in the opening chapter the need to have a narrative – an overriding explanation of why this project needs to be done and what the overall benefit is. We also need to drill down a bit further and quantify these benefits. This is important because we need to be able to justify the cost of the project. That doesn't necessarily mean we'll spend £1m and over five years realise benefits of £5m; it's rarely that simple. There are other drivers that require projects to deliver specific outcomes, such as legislative changes or commercial contracts coming to an end, etc. However, if an organisation is going to spend a significant amount of money and time, then really it needs to be able to spell out quantifiable benefits to justify this. When I said 'it' in that last sentence, I of course meant you.

The scale and scope of a project will have an impact on how much time and effort should go into the benefits side of things. For large-scale national public-sector projects and programmes, there should be a business case that will include a large section on the benefits which underpin the rationale for the project.

But whether in the public or private sector, any project will be subject to challenge over its lifetime. Prevailing winds change and what seemed like a good idea 18 months ago now might not. Or more likely still, people come and go, including the original project sponsors, and you can easily find no one's actually sure why this project ever seemed like a good idea in the first place. This last scenario happens a lot.

You're the PM, you're putting your heart and soul into this project, and you believe in it. You'd better be able to spell out exactly why when the challenges start coming.

In an ideal world, you'd step into a project and the business would have already worked out the benefits case. It would all add up perfectly; you'd just need to deliver, and the benefits would take care of themselves. More likely, though, there'll be some benefits alluded to somewhere but they'll be a bit abstract and no one will ever be able to measure whether they happened or not. HS2, the UK high-speed rail link, suffers from this problem. The benefits of it aren't clear beyond reducing journey times, which is good – but how is the country better off because of this? The failure to clearly spell this out is one reason why it's under constant threat of being axed.

So it's incumbent on you as PM to dig into those initial business drivers, make sense of them and potentially elaborate them.

'It's just obviously a good idea.'

Is it? I worked on the NHS Summary Care Record programme. This was a huge national undertaking to make patients' information from electronic GP records nationally available. The key benefit people always used to talk about was that if you were from Newcastle but were taken ill on holiday in Newquay, then the local hospital could see your GP-held information — meaning you'd get better care. Seems to make sense, doesn't it? Except if you looked at the figures from accident and emergency departments in the south west of England, you'd see that well over 80% of the patients they see are from that area. Is it still such a good idea?

A better case (which was made and delivered on) was that out-of-hours care rarely had access to patient information even when the patient was local, and that hospital pharmacists couldn't reconcile patients' medications without calling the GP. So, in fact, the Summary Care Record was a good idea, but you can see the danger in making the wrong case based on easily disproved assumptions.

Assuming we've got our basic assumptions right, we then need to drill down and get some measurable information.

I ran a discovery phase for a genomics project looking at introducing a national digital solution for test ordering and results delivery. Genomics is cutting-edge science which has the capacity to radically change the way healthcare is delivered in the UK. However, there was no standard way of ordering a test. Requests used a mix of long-winded manual processes, email and some local automation. So introducing a national system for standardising all this and getting off paper systems was again 'obviously a good idea, right?' Well, yes, it was — but we still needed to be able to state why and measure it. Actually, this was quite straightforward. We asked: how many test requests are currently rejected because of incomplete data? How many are illegible? Or used the wrong order form? How much time is spent dealing with these rejected tests? How much time is spent keying this information into different systems? What's the cost of all this? With a bit of research and persistence, we could start to build quite a compelling benefits model for a digital solution that would slash these costs.

So be prepared to get into the detail. You don't have to stand over someone with a stopwatch timing how long it takes them to transcribe data from a paper form, but some idea of the scale of the current shortcomings will really help.

Make sure you're pitching the benefits at the right level too. When looking at the potential benefits of procuring a replacement national email system for the NHS, we briefly looked at how much paper and postage would be saved. This was silly – no one in their right mind would suggest a large organisation ditch email and go back to writing hard-copy letters. No, the benefits case was based around the cost saving of procuring one national system rather than maintaining any number of local systems.

Identifying benefits isn't the same as realising them. This is where things get very murky. Benefits are almost certainly going to take years to be realised. By that point, the project team will be long gone. Yes, in an ideal world we'd have perfectly baselined the current costs and then be able to see them falling over a period of years. Really it's down to the business, possibly the SRO, to take responsibility for measuring the benefits post project, but I've never known this to happen properly. So identify them, cost them, learn them off by heart – but don't put too much time into measuring them post project. Others may disagree, and maybe I'm wrong on this. But when did you last see a benefits realisation role advertised?

No matter how good your planning skills are, or how great you are at managing risks and issues, and even if you're the best report writer in the world and a total natural when it comes to leadership, if you can't manage your stakeholders, you won't manage your project.

You'll often hear the term 'stakeholder engagement' bandied about, but I think that's a misnomer. It's not just about engaging with different project stakeholders, it's about proactively managing them. I don't mean in the same way that you manage your team; this is about finding ways to communicate with people connected with your project, and influencing them to do (or perhaps not do) things which may help (or hinder) your project's chances of success. This more than any other single trait is the key to being a great project manager, and it will set you apart from your peers if you can crack it.

Firstly, you need to work out who your stakeholders are. This will change over the course of the project, as you'll constantly come across different people who might be able to help you. But you've got to start somewhere. If I was after a definition, I'd say it was anyone involved in your project who sits outside your formal reporting structure.

A stakeholder map is a good place to start. Draw a graph with an x and y axis. Along the y axis, plot level of interest (you don't need an actual scale) from 'not interested' to 'very interested', and then along the x axis plot 'not influential' to 'very influential'. All you then need to do is start putting names on the graph.

Your potential suppliers will be very interested and probably quite influential so will be close to top right on the graph. The users will be reasonably interested but not that influential, so they'll be nearer top left. How about an outgoing supplier who's out of the frame for the future? Not that interested, but quite influential (you'll need them on side when you migrate to the new system): bottom right maybe? Hopefully you get the idea.

Now, although I don't think you should use this as a formal tool, it will help you think about how to communicate. We want the users on side, but we can't invest too much time on them at this stage (they'll move to the top right when we're going live), so maybe go and address one of their team meetings to let them know what's happening? Potential suppliers – well, they need a lot of time invested. Maybe start planning a supplier engagement event, and get the whole team involved. The incumbent supplier? There'll be some sensitivities there, and it's unlikely they'll want to come to too many meetings with a customer that's leaving. But you can't leave them out of the loop. Maybe keep an informal channel open with your contact, pick up the phone and go for the occasional coffee?

Another good reason for doing the above exercise is that it might stop you failing to recognise an important stakeholder – or, rather, failing to recognise their influence …

I've already mentioned being PM on a programme to introduce a new coding system in England's GP estate. To my mind, this was really between the organisation that I was working for – NHS Digital – and the four GP system suppliers who would deliver the changes. By this stage, I thought of myself as an old hand at this type of programme, and I was keen to avoid what I saw as a lot of unnecessary time talking to groups and bodies who wouldn't offer any help (there's a lot of this in the NHS). Top of this list was the grandly titled Joint GP Information Technology Committee (JGPITC) – a group of GPs with an interest in IT, made up of members from the Royal College of GPs and the BMA (hence the 'Joint'). I'd spent many a fun time presenting to this group before: you stand before their horseshoe arrangement of desks as if on trial, while they make withering observations about what you're doing. Pointless in my opinion. So I was happy to let this slide and strike a blow against officialdom.

The rest writes itself, doesn't it? They got in touch: they knew about the programme, they weren't looped in and they didn't like it. They had the channels and the ability to write to every GP in the country expressing concerns about the whole approach, which I've no doubt they would have done had we not changed tack. Stick that on your risks and issues log …

So the lesson to be learnt here is get your stakeholders at the right point on the graph. Just because a person or group doesn't seem that interested or influential, it doesn't mean they aren't. Even if you don't think a stakeholder can offer you any help, it doesn't mean they can't do you a lot of harm.

The postscript to this is that we really worked on that relationship with the JGPITC. We seconded four of their members onto the project team as advisors, and never missed a single meeting again, smiling through it all rather than scowling. They did eventually write their letter too – an extremely supportive one.

Suppliers are an interesting kind of stakeholder. But whether they're on their way out, on their way in, or are an incumbent who'll be there for a long time to come, you must treat them as stakeholders and not just as organisations that you have a contractual relationship with. If you reach for the contract when you disagree about something, then they'll do the same and you'll never get anywhere. Contracts in my experience are never particularly clear cut in any case, and if you end up arguing over them, the relationship has already broken down.

So how should you manage such disagreements? Well, firstly, try and see the world from the supplier's point of view. Even if you feel they aren't delivering what they should, that doesn't mean they're the enemy or that they're taking some strange pleasure in making your life difficult. The person you're dealing with is probably struggling with their technical team, or their manager may be giving them conflicting messages, and you're just one of many problems they're dealing with (you should go for a drink – you'd probably get on). So you need to get your relationship to an open and honest point where you can be frank about problems without coming over as though you're telling them off. (After all, how do *you* like being spoken to like that? Does it bring out the best in you?)

You need to develop a rapport. You can't do that by email, and I'd suggest you can't do it by timetabled Zoom/Teams calls. You need to pick up the phone, and you need to make sure they know they can pick up the phone to you too. Supplier conflicts come from miscommunication more than anything else, so if you're communicating well that's half the battle. You can also say things over the phone that maybe you wouldn't write down or say in a meeting. Saying, 'Look, maybe this wasn't that clear and I'm sorry about that ...' can go a long way towards building trust. Some of this may seem obvious but most people don't do it.

Just to be clear, these informal channels aren't a substitute for more formal ones. You still need proper meetings with actions, and so on.

The real key to managing your suppliers (and, in fact, all your stakeholders) is trying to align what you both want to get out of the project. Do they really just want to deliver the bare minimum and move on to something else? Is that so bad if they do? If you can agree on what that bare minimum is, then great, and you can plan your engagement accordingly with well spelt-out requirements and light-touch meeting schedules.

Or if they want this to be a flagship project for them, again that may really work for you. In this case, you'd be looking for a much more involved collaborative approach. Some information about the state of the company might help here. Are they a new market entrant looking to make a splash, or have they been around a long time and are losing customers? All this will inform the way they behave.

Tip: Don't fall into the trap of focusing on the supplier you've ended up being matey with. Those relationships that are a bit more stilted need just as much attention from you, and, strangely, they'll be the ones who'll end up coming through for you. Note – this is true for team members too.

So you want to know who all your stakeholders are at the beginning, but this list will evolve over the course of the project so do keep updating your graph. Also, be on the lookout for people who might not be an obvious stakeholder right now but who could become one further down the line. That service person who joined a couple of early calls but then disappeared as it was too early for their involvement … It'll be well worth keeping a channel open with them as you'll need them later. Also, remember people move around and change jobs. By the time you go live, that service person might now be service director – and they know you!

What I'm trying to get at here is that you need to really grow your network – and that doesn't mean just connecting with people on LinkedIn. That's not real; it's a substitute for an actual network (though it will come in handy when you're job hunting). Even if the contacts you make can't help you on this project, there'll be others.

If your project lends itself to it, then conferences or engagement events are a great way to not only spread the word but develop new contacts. If you're presenting (and you should be), then make sure you're available afterwards. I can guarantee people will approach you for a chat.

I realise this approach doesn't suit everyone, and it can be difficult and sometimes go wrong. But if you can develop this slightly pushy side to your game, it will bring huge benefits to the project and to you individually. Also, remember you've got a team – encourage them to seek out potential stakeholders too.

Lastly, you will often see communication and stakeholder engagement grouped together. This is mistake in my opinion. Yes, some comms resource might be useful if you're on a high-profile project where there's likely to be a lot of external communications. They can help you draft comms releases and suggest approaches. They may well have some useful contacts and channels you can exploit. But (and I know this is a recurring theme) you're the PM, and managing your stakeholders is on you.

No matter the scale of your project, you're going to need a process for handling, storing and updating all the project controls and other documentation. Most importantly, you're going to need someone to manage this. Get this right and you'll save yourself a LOT of stress. Get it wrong and it will end up consuming you, and you won't have time to manage your stakeholders, your team and everything else.

Over the course of a typical week, you'll be asked for information from all sorts of different people and departments: Finance, Audit, your manager, etc. If you have to start scrabbling around for this information only to find it's out of date, that's not good, is it? You should be on top of all this information in any case.

So you need a process for making sure the information is always up to date. First, you need to have a common document store that the whole team can access. It doesn't really matter what or how as long as there is one. Obviously, it needs to be logically set out with some way of versioning documents, and you then need a system for reviewing and updating them.

But what you really need is a project management office manager – a 'PMO'. Their job is to set up and organise the document store, produce the plans, organise the project board, ensure the risks and issues are up to date and, ideally, be your therapist.

So who do you have as the PMO? I've been very lucky to work with some very good ones. They tend to have a slightly controlling personality, enjoy updating plans, love spreadsheets and take a real pride in everything being up to date. This is exactly what you're looking for. It's not a junior PM who's got lumped with it when they really want to be doing something else. It's someone with a decent amount of experience who can help come up with mitigations for risks and suggestions for plans, etc. It may seem like I'm labouring this, but to some extent this person really needs to be your second in command. But remember, they'll go on holiday, they'll be off sick, they may even leave. So make sure you're up to speed with everything. Yes, they'll do the leg work, but you aren't delegating it away.

Tip: Project support officers (PSOs – but terms may vary) tend to be used in different ways on projects, from booking train tickets to managing stakeholder engagement events. Making them responsible for elements of the PMO role is good experience for them and will you give some resilience when your PMO manager goes on holiday or follows through on a threat to leave.

Schedule in a weekly meeting with your PMO and stick to it. There'll always be a temptation to bump this one first when your diary starts to get crowded – but resist this. Then you need to go through every risk and issue, all your finance spreadsheets, the plan and everything else.

Just a note on the finances: you must always be on top of your numbers. What's the overall cost of the project? How are we doing against this projection? Under? Over? What are we doing about that? Where are we with getting our funding agreed? How much does the team cost per month? Is the team at full strength? What are the financial benefits? Unless you're an accountant, this probably doesn't come naturally to you so you need to make it easy for yourself. Have a dashboard for all these matters. It's completely reasonable for anyone to ask any of these questions at any time. Make sure you don't have to respond with: 'Can I get back to you?'

Hopefully you can see this is really about getting organised, and getting into good habits that will help you avoid panicked responses.

Leadership and management aren't the same thing, but they do overlap.

In the leadership section of this chapter, I'll look at the specific behaviours and characteristics that you need to adopt to become a good leader.

In the management section, I'll focus more on the nuts and bolts of how to organise and manage your team, as well as yourself and your boss.

Leadership

If you're ever asked in an interview what the most important element of project management is, this is the correct response:

'Strong leadership, both in terms of the project team and the wider stakeholders, is the most essential element to a project's success. I believe a lack of this is why many projects fail. What I mean by leadership is that I can create an environment where people feel driven and able to contribute, but I expect to be ultimately responsible for decisions and the project's successes and failures.'

You do need to remember to include failures at the end or you'll risk sounding arrogant.

There have been volumes written about leadership. There are a thousand courses you can go on to learn it, improve upon it, or even just give up and accept you've either got it or you haven't (this isn't true). Everyone needs to develop their own style of leadership, deriving from the kind of person they are. If you're a quiet introvert, that's fine. Some of the best people I've worked for have exuded a quiet confidence. More the loud, outgoing type? That's ok too. You can get along with everyone, and people won't want to miss your team meetings. Different types of people all have their pros and cons, and actually different phases of a project might require different leadership styles.

But the one thing you will always notice about leadership, far more than any particular style, is an absence of it.

I'm not going to try and tell you how to be a great leader, but I do think there are certain behaviours that you must master to lead a project well.

Firstly, you must accept that you do need to provide leadership. The role of PM isn't just to make sure all the risks and issues are logged, that the plans are up to date and all the workstreams are reporting progress. You need to be the focal point of things. Decisions need to flow through you. You're the face of the project. Most of all, your team expect this. People need and want to be led.

Now, a common trap with this is falling into control freakery. We've all worked for someone who concerns themselves with the minutiae of every workstream, who rewrites every document, who leads on every meeting, etc. This is the quickest way to have a mutinous team and disenfranchised stakeholders. On the other hand, being too above the fray will make you too distant from what's going on. There are no magic formulae on getting the balance right but with a bit of experience you should find the right level.

That coding programme I worked on for the NHS is a case in point. The programme's subject matter – a terminology called SNOMED CT – is incredibly complex in terms of how it works and how it's structured. The experts, known as terminologists, are usually people with a medical background and years of experience in the subject. So, even if I'd had the time (and brains) to get up to a good level of understanding on it, and then started wading in on their esoteric discussions, how would that have gone down with them? Badly, obviously. Then again, how about if I'd just left them to it? 'Just let me know when it's all working and we can roll it out – thanks!' That doesn't really work either, does it?

A middle ground then: 'Give me a few delivery milestones and I can report on them ...' But the PMO could say that. You're the PM and you're supposed to be in charge.

How about spending some time with the terminologists and showing interest in this seemingly impenetrable discipline, so that you can eventually surface the elements that you do need to understand and work out what needs to happen to resolve or deliver them? With any specialised area this isn't easy. It's frustrating and it might well mean you have to stretch your brain a bit more than you want to.

It also might leave you feeling a bit exposed. To be able to deal with this you need confidence ...

What does confidence really mean? The ability to come across well in meetings? To be good at presenting to a roomful of people? To always have the answer to every question? To be great in front of senior management? We've all met people who can do all these things – and we've also all been taken in by people who can seemingly do all these things.

I'd say confidence in this example is the ability to admit that you don't know things. And you need your team to give you the confidence that either you don't need to know about that particular thing or that they can give you enough information about it.

But it's actually more than that. You can't lead a team of people without a level of personal confidence, and this is something most people need to work at. I actually believe that being able to project confidence is one of the most important elements of leadership. If you aren't confident yourself, you won't be able to inspire confidence in others.

Think of a meeting you've been in where the PM is obviously not getting the information they need from the team. People are being evasive; it looks like someone's not done what they were supposed to do. The PM's snapping and being tetchy, perhaps even losing their temper, and you can see why. They have good reason. But it's not a good look, is it? Surely, they can take this more in their stride? Why do they get so wound up?

Same scenario, different PM. Still the information isn't forthcoming. This time, though, no one's being challenged; it's all just being accepted as if it's of no consequence. Why is this all seemingly ok? Why isn't the PM pushing back?

Both responses betray a lack of confidence. In the first case, the PM feels undermined and maybe lacking in respect from the team, and they're now worried about having to report a lack of progress up. In the second case, the PM isn't confident enough to challenge. Perhaps they feel out of their depth and are worried challenging will just expose their lack of knowledge.

Now, in both these examples, particularly the latter, being on top of the project in terms of deliverables and plans should help head these situations off at the pass. Inevitability, though, such situations will still occur at times, as will a host of other problems when it's all going wrong (which it will). So you need to develop a confident demeanour.

How? First of all, you need to get on top your body language. Body language gives as much away as anything you say (and more according to some studies). So jabbing your finger and shaking your head (first scenario) or sinking further into your chair and wringing your hands (second scenario) are all out.

You need to look people in the eye, and not roll yours. Adopt a straight posture. Watch what your hands are doing. Speak clearly and directly in a neutral tone. Don't be afraid to challenge – it's expected of you – but keep it measured and non-accusatory. If nothing else, you can always become a professional poker player if the project management thing doesn't work out.

This needs a lot of practice.

Tip: You must never under any circumstances whatsoever lose your temper. Many years ago, I shouted at someone in an open-plan office. They seemed to be going out of their way to be obstructive and had been for weeks. I immediately apologised and hoped it would be forgotten. Four years later, I was chatting to someone vaguely connected with the event. 'Still can't believe that time you lost your temper with xxxx.' They weren't even there! No one will ever remember the rights and wrongs or what led to your outburst; they'll just remember you lost your temper and judge you for it. If you feel yourself about to explode, immediately leave the office and go for a walk round the block.

A key part of project leadership is making good decisions. This doesn't mean making snap ones. I said at the beginning of this section that decisions need to flow through you. This doesn't mean you alone must make decisions, but as the PM you do need to be able to get the right people together, ensure you've got enough information, and facilitate a good debate on the pros and cons of different options. You're looking to arrive at a consensus which you can then stand behind.

Tip: Just to be slightly contrary here, you do need to make lower-level decisions quickly or you'll come over as flaky. When do you need the plans by? Who needs to be at this workshop? Can this risk be closed? If you turn everything into a debate, you'll get a reputation as someone who can't make a decision. And that's right up there with being a bad driver and lacking a sense of humour.

A few other leadership attributes worth mentioning:

You must treat everyone the same. You can't play favourites within the team or externally. Of course you'd rather spend the last hour on Friday catching up with that person who's on the same wavelength as you. But that person who's a bit snarky with you still needs your time. People will notice if you don't treat everyone equally and it breeds resentment.

You need to be reasonably serious. I know I said at the beginning of this chapter that you should be yourself, and that's true. However, if you fancy yourself as a bit of a comedian, good for you, but rein it in. Don't lose it completely – it's a great strength that'll work wonders for stakeholder engagement and team morale. But it can soon start to grate, and you can easily undermine yourself if you employ it too much.

Running a tight ship with a tight command-and-control ethos doesn't work. You want a collegial environment where everyone feels able to contribute and express themselves and challenge you. Don't let your ego get in the way of this.

Give people the benefit of the doubt. Very few are out to do a bad job or make your life difficult.

Perhaps the most important attribute of all is integrity. So be honest and consistent in your dealings with people. Do the right thing in the right way (I don't need to tell you what that is; you already know). Don't think being Machiavellian ever works. It will always blow up in your face. It didn't even really work for Machiavelli – he was thrown in prison and tortured.

But you do need to be politically savvy. Know what your boss wants, and understand their pressures. Be aware of stakeholders' different agendas. Use that knowledge to inform your communications with them.

Lastly, be aware that none of the above just applies to your leadership role with your team. It's crucial that your leadership skills are used to good effect across the whole project landscape: with suppliers, senior management, users, and so on. Once you've done that, you've cracked project leadership. (Note – no one has ever completely cracked project leadership.)

Management

Managing people is difficult. People are complex: they have needs, fears, goals, ambitions – just like you. Perhaps the most important point to bear in mind is that you're not always going to get it right. You're going to recruit the wrong person at some point, put your foot in it with somebody, task someone with a job which in retrospect was obviously not suited to their skillset, accidentally undermine someone. Don't beat yourself up when this happens. Learn from it though.

So with that in mind, I've split this section into recruitment and then managing the team, managing yourself and managing up.

Recruitment

So who's on the team? In an ideal world, you'd start with a blank page and be able to recruit exactly who you wanted, thus ensuring the perfect blend of skills and personality types to deliver the project. This never happens. You're almost certainly going to get what you're given, at least initially.

Over time, though, people will leave and the project's team will require a change in its make-up as you progress, so you will have a chance to bring in people of your own choosing. It's important to take a step back when you think you need some new resources. For example, if the technical architect is leaving, you probably need to whistle up another one with as close a skills match as possible, right? Well, maybe. But on the other hand, were you getting what you needed from the outgoing one? Perhaps a lot of the thinking on the technical side has been agreed now and so you need someone with more implementation experience. What do others in the team think? Don't be afraid to shuffle the pack. If you've got the budget, it's up to you to decide what the resource profile needs to be.

Once you've decided what role you need filling, you're then into recruitment, and it's crucial to start early. There'll likely be some internal HR processes to navigate, and you may need to advertise internally before you can look externally. Then you have to schedule the interviews and allow for people being on leave, etc. Best possible case is three months, start to finish. So you need to get on with the process quickly or you'll end up with a huge gap between someone leaving and the new person coming in.

First of all, when you write the job specification, keep it as high level as possible without being completely generic. You don't want to put people off who might not be completely perfect but could do the job. On the other hand, you don't want to have to sift through hundreds of applications. (It's worth emphasising here that someone in the team should be doing this alongside you.)

Once you've got your shortlist, it's time for interviews – a potential minefield. Competency-based interviews have been in vogue for quite a long time. There is something in having sets of questions which relate to specific competencies, and being able to score candidates' answers accordingly. The winner becomes whoever gets the most points. Straightforward, right? Except it isn't. Will this person fit into the team? Are they a good fit for your organisation's wider culture? Can you imagine them being helpful with a difficult supplier? This is all very difficult to ascertain by asking a series of closed questions. You're going to have to come to your own conclusions based on how they act, speak and generally present themselves. It's crucial therefore that you interview with someone you can trust and who's on the same page as you in terms of who'll fit in. Then at the end of the interview session, you can compare your initial draft scores and adjust accordingly to ensure you get the right person. Do this and your process will be completely auditable.

Your job is to build a team who can deliver the project while keeping within the letter of your organisation's recruitment policies. It isn't to dogmatically stick to a process that you had no say in and that may not give you what you want at the end of it. Trust your instincts when it comes to interviews. You'll usually be right. And if you can't find the right person? Don't appoint.

Tip: This will happen to you ... You interview a few people, one person obviously stands out and so you make them an offer. However, you can really imagine one of the other candidates in the team – perhaps not quite in this role, or maybe they were only just beaten into second place. Why not take another look at your budget and your resource profile? Can you find a way to get this person in? How about a chat with your boss? Maybe they've got some budget they could let you have? Maybe there's some scope to create a secondment opportunity? Good people are really difficult to find so it's always worth using your imagination to try and get them even if they weren't first choice for the original role.

If all the above sounds like too much hard work, well, there is another option: reach for a contractor. This is a temporary person, provided by an external consultancy or recruited directly by you, paid for on a day-rate basis. Contractors provide flexibility: you can take them on for a specific time frame, and you don't normally have to go through a fixed recruitment process. (This doesn't mean that you treat them any differently to the rest of the team. I worked somewhere once where contractors had to wear different coloured ID-card lanyards, and it didn't do much for team coherence.)

That said, you'll be paying a significant day rate for these people, and you should feel you're getting your money's worth. This doesn't mean they're out the door at the first sign of a mistake. But it does mean that if they aren't performing, you need feel no compunction in not renewing their contract or even letting them go early. The latter is generally seen as poor form so it's best to offer a short three-month contract initially and then you're covered if it's not working out.

Managing the team

To have a successful project team, it's crucial that everyone feels invested in the project's outcomes, that they've bought into the mission and understand the part they're playing in it. This won't happen automatically – it's something you need to work on both initially and throughout the project's lifetime. This is where your management skills are really needed. You need to be able to communicate well and make sure people understand exactly what's required of them. Most of all, though, you need to support them.

Firstly then, does everyone know what the mission is? There's no point you working hard to understand the project fundamentals if there are 10 different perceptions within the project team. So I'd suggest, once you've got up to speed yourself, you sit down with the team and test everyone's understanding. Discuss it, taking as long as is needed. If you don't find agreement at this point it will become a problem down the line.

I was involved once in what should have been a short discovery piece on making some potential changes to a clinical application. However, the service designer had a much grander vision of what we were trying to achieve. We never really reconciled this, which led to a fractious project team and a poor project outcome. You can't shy away from potentially difficult conversations where ultimately you have to tell someone they're on the wrong track (once you're sure *you* aren't).

Tip: Once you've got everyone on the same page, develop a slide pack which pulls everything together: what you're doing and why, and how you're going to deliver it. Then give everyone in the team an opportunity to present it. At the early stage of the project there should be plenty of scope for delivering this to different groups, e.g. the wider department team meetings and user group meetings, etc. Obviously, you'll need to match experience with the audience, but in giving even the most junior person in the team this responsibility, you're showing that you trust them and you're reinforcing that they're a crucial part of the team.

As well as the project outcomes, people need to know exactly which elements they're responsible for. This sounds obvious but unless it's completely spelt out at the start, that one-degree difference in alignment will mean you're a mile out in six months' time. So, again, discuss openly with the team, remember to be collegial, but do be firm about what you want to get from these discussions.

You should be setting individual objectives for six to 12 months which are linked to the project deliverables. It's important to discuss and agree these as you both need to buy into them. Make sure they contain enough detail to ensure it's clear what the objective is – you can't have any ambiguity here. Keep reviewing them regularly too. Whatever you do, don't wait until the six or 12-month period is up before you dust them off to see how it's gone.

The most important part of team communication is making sure people understand what you actually want them to do – not just in the case of long-term deliverables but in the more short-term day-to-day stuff too. This doesn't mean everything needs to be spelt out to the nth degree; it does mean making sure they know exactly what you're expecting and when. In my opinion, these seemingly obvious points are where things usually fall down. I've lost count of the catch-ups I've had with team members where they don't seem to have progressed a task, or what they've done isn't really what I thought I'd asked for. This has inevitably led to me feeling let down and them feeling confused about my ill-disguised disappointment ... But virtually every time it was my fault for not being clearer in the first place.

This isn't solved by issuing edicts for everything you ever want done. It's solved by having a meaningful conversation where you can both check your understanding without the team member worrying they aren't getting it and without you blithely assuming everything you say makes complete sense to everyone else.

I do think it's important to get to know your team beyond the work side of things (within reason). If someone's got a lot going on at home, then it's better you know so that at least on some level you can support them, cut them a bit of slack and provide cover where required. But even on a more day-to-day level, what are their hobbies? How many kids do they have? Where are they going on holiday? You're going to spend a lot of time with these people; life will be a lot better if you're on friendly terms.

Be aware, though, that however great a boss you are, someone you gave a great opportunity to and supported through thick and thin will eventually decide they hate you. Don't take it personally. That's life.

In terms of managing the team on a week-by-week basis, you should be having one-to-ones every week with your direct reports. This needs to go beyond long and short-term deliverables and objectives. You want to know how they are. How was that holiday? Is everything generally ok? Things will naturally move to work specifics. This absolutely isn't about them assuring you everything's on track and you either blindly accepting that or trying to pick holes in what they're telling you; it's about having an open and honest conversation. You also need some continuity to these conversations: it's important if they've mentioned something one week that you pick it up with them the next. If they've got people reporting to them, find out how they're getting on. Most importantly, you want to know how you can help with any problems.

Make sure they understand that they have access to you whenever they need it. You don't want to wait until you have a scheduled call before interacting with your team.

Regrettably, you're going to have to deal with poor performance at some point. This isn't something you can duck. We've covered contractors but if it's a permanent employee, then you need to offer support and opportunities to improve. In my experience, if people aren't performing it's usually because they aren't in quite the right role for them. But that doesn't mean they can't grow into that role. So keep it informal at first. Is there anything you can help with? Can anyone else in the team help? Or someone from another team? It's crucial that you do everything in your power to support people who are struggling, as a) it's just the right thing to do, and b) if things do have to become more formal you've shown that you tried your best to fix things.

You should have a weekly team meeting, and everyone should understand that this is a priority. I'd suggest having it mid-week as this is a good point to take stock, when people are in the thick of the issues. You're looking to create a friendly, informal atmosphere where everyone feels able to contribute. In fact, it's important that everyone does contribute, so make sure you go round the room and give everyone a chance to speak. Also, give everyone's issues equal time. People not filling in the leave rota properly might not be as important as the go-live date disappearing over the horizon, but it is to whoever's trying to keep the leave rota up to date. So don't shoo these issues away, and make sure you back up the junior team members.

So in order to be a great manager, be clear about what you want, be proactive not reactive, keep talking to your team and keep looking for opportunities to support them. This all takes time and effort (and practice), but it's a crucial element of the job, not a nice-to-have when you're on top of everything else.

Managing yourself
This is an often-overlooked element of management but if you can't manage your own time and behaviour, you're unlikely to be able to manage anyone else.

We've all come across that character at work who's some kind of genius but is obviously disorganised, turns up late for meetings, never has the right papers, and is always distracted. Now, if you're also a genius, good on you and you can probably get away with being like this too. If not, though, a slightly shambolic air isn't endearing; it's annoying – and alarming even.

This is really about professionalism. You need to project a professional image, and you're unlikely to be able to do that if you're turning up late for meetings and can't remember the SRO's name. There isn't one overriding attribute or skill to learn and practise in managing yourself, so below I've set out some thoughts and pointers which may help.

Firstly, know your own strengths and weaknesses, and be honest with yourself about them. We've already mentioned finance and I think this is a real blind spot for a lot of people. It doesn't always help that you may well be inheriting someone else's system of spreadsheets for tracking it all.

Now, acknowledging a weakness isn't compensating for it. You can't just say, 'I'm not really a finance person,' and get someone else to do it. You need to find a way to manage that element that works for you. Work with your PMO to simplify the way the data's presented, diarise time with the accountant regularly and stick to it. But also confront the thing you're not very good at. Challenge yourself to improve. You *can* work out the finances; they're unlikely to really be that complicated. In fact, be honest – you just don't like doing it.

So that's weaknesses. How about strengths? Maybe you love presenting – working up an imaginative slide deck, delivering it to a roomful of people, handling the questions with panache. Good for you, that's a great skill. But you can't spend your whole time doing this. There's no point going on the conference circuit, telling everyone how great it will be when your project delivers, if in fact it will never be delivered because no one's managing it. Don't just focus on the things you enjoy.

Get on top of your diary. People love telling everyone else how 'back to back' their diaries are. The move to remote working has led to this idea that diaries should just be one conference call after another. There's no reason for this; this isn't how projects were running pre-March 2020. It may be to do with presenteeism, i.e. proving you're doing something, or it may be showing off to whoever you share your house with just how important you are. Whatever the reasons, you can't let your day be organised around meeting after meeting, many of which have just morphed into scheduled calls without any obvious purpose. It's completely unproductive.

So have the confidence to thin your diary out. Only schedule and attend meetings that you can add value to and get value from. (Remember though to keep an eye on the politics – it should be obvious which meetings this applies to.) Block out time to stop random people adding meetings in. Always check ahead in your diary to see what's coming in the next week, and particularly tomorrow, that you need to be really on top of. Don't just turn up to meetings without being prepped or without having a clear idea of what you want to get out of it.

That last point holds true for many encounters at work. Think about what you want to get out of that call you're about to have with, say, a supplier. You need to know about a problem they're supposed to be fixing, so how are you going to frame the question? What's their response likely to be? How are you going to react if it's bad news? Then what? Just spending a couple of minutes thinking about how encounters are likely to play out can really improve your performance.

Make sure you find some thinking time. If you aren't reflecting on what you're doing and how you're doing it, then you won't be effective as you'll only ever be dealing with what's immediately in front of you. Train journeys are great for this.

Don't make a big show of how busy you are. You'll just come across as stressed. If you're on holiday or a training course, then you're not contactable. Otherwise people don't know whether to expect a response or not.

You don't have to be the first to arrive and last to leave every day. But you do sometimes. You certainly can't be the last to arrive and first to leave, ever.

Don't procrastinate boring, fiddly tasks. In fact, do them first. You'll feel better about yourself and won't get into trouble for being six months late with your expenses claims.

Do buy the first round of drinks at the team night out. Don't make a drunken fool of yourself.

Managing up

You may get some say over who's in your team. But you'll never get to choose your boss.

Hopefully, you'll go through your whole career reporting to people who are reasonable and supportive, and who like you and get where you're coming from. More likely though, you're going to have to deal with a whole range of personality types, from the mild mannered to the seemingly deranged. Whatever they're like as a person, they aren't going to change to suit you so you're going to have to work out how to work with them.

The starting point must be to work out what your boss wants from you. Not just in terms of formal reporting and project outputs, but do they want to be looped into everything or just by exception? Do they want to attend team meetings? How much control of the board do they want? And so on.

Bear in mind that at the beginning your boss probably doesn't know you. They're going to need time to work out how much autonomy they're comfortable giving you. This is completely reasonable – they're on the hook for delivering this too. So don't feel too put out if you feel a bit over-managed in these early stages.

You certainly should ensure they're invited to early planning sessions and ongoing team meetings. Again, don't get resentful if it feels like they're taking over in these meetings. They'll have their opinions informed by their own experiences. Yes, maybe they're trying to establish the pecking order a bit too. Just go with the flow and don't react. People will see what's going on and it will reflect well on you if you handle it maturely.

Tip: Even if your boss doesn't require a weekly formal report, do send them an email on Fridays with a roundup of what's happened in the week. They'll appreciate it.

It's going to take time to develop a good, trusting relationship with your boss. The most important thing you can do to speed this up is give them transparency of what's happening with the project. We've already looked at reporting but that shouldn't be the only conduit. You need to be having a catch-up every week, perhaps using the formal report as a basis for discussion. But really you want to get to a point where you can pick up the phone as and when ...

... But do this without becoming needy. Don't cc them into every email that you send or over-escalate issues. Always try and solve things yourself first.

... But don't under-escalate either. Never get to a point where you're not letting your boss know about a serious issue. This will be bad enough when you have to belatedly break it to them, but many times worse if they are blindsided with it from another source, perhaps their boss. Putting them in a very exposed spot like this will likely make them tighten up on the level of autonomy they're prepared to give you.

Obviously, this is a difficult balance to get right and there's bound to be a few hiccups at first. But keep talking. Ask the question: 'Are you getting what you need from me?' Make it easy for them to give you feedback, which will benefit you both.

Tip: Rather than cc-ing them into every email exchange that you think might be worth flagging, just forward emails on to them with a 'FYI. Don't need you to do anything here, just giving you a heads-up'.

There's bound to come a point when they make a decision you don't agree with. It's absolutely part of your job to challenge this. Make sure, though, that you have this conversation privately. If it gets played out in front of the team, a) they may feel undermined, and b) there's a good chance their position will become more entrenched. Make your points clearly, logically and calmly. If they do come round to your way of thinking, you need to find a way to badge this as a compromise position rather than a 'win' for you. If they don't, then no matter how wrong you think the decision is, you need to get behind it and support it to the team and the wider stakeholders. Never be tempted to go over your boss's head. How would you like that?

To conclude, your relationship with your boss is probably your key one. Take time to get it right by building trust, showing them respect and making their life easier. Bear in mind they'll have other direct reports, some of whom at least won't be behaving like this.

Get it right and you'll have a great ally.

Speaking to a roomful of people probably fills you with dread – that's a completely natural reaction. It's how most people feel, even the ones who seem good at it. However, almost certainly as a PM you're going to have to do it quite a lot, so it's a skill worth mastering.

Most people approach presentations by pulling a slide deck together with the relevant facts and figures, standing up and reading out the slides as rapidly as possible, asking for questions at the end, looking surprised but relieved when there aren't any, and then quickly sitting back down again. How many presentations have you sat though like this? They weren't very inspiring, were they? Were you even still listening after slide two?

To get better at presentations, the first thing is to stop viewing them as an ordeal to get through. Try and embrace the chance to tell people about your project and convey whatever message you want to get over.

What is that message? Well, that depends on why you've been asked to present. Quite often I've been asked to present at conference-type events where the audience may have a general interest in your project. So are they really likely to want to know at what point in your project timeline you're planning on going into regression testing? Will many of them even know what regression testing is? In that instance, boil your presentation down to a few key points. Set the scene: what's the problem? How is your project going to fix it? By when? This is a great chance to sell the benefits. Don't have too many slides – this is nearly always a mistake. Four or five is as many as you need, with just a few lines on each. They're just there to frame what you're saying; if they're too busy you'll lose people.

Now, if your audience happens to be the Royal Society of Regression Testers, then certainly focus on the regression testing element, but do so as part of the overall big-picture narrative. This approach does mean your delivery is going to have to step up a gear – you can't just read out from the slides. But that doesn't mean you should be ad-libbing; you need to know what you're going to say at each point. The trick is to make it *look* like you're ad-libbing. (There may well come a point when you can speak well off the cuff from a few slides, but don't risk that until you're absolutely confident you can carry it off).

When you come to actually delivering the presentation, ensure beforehand that the equipment is there and your slide deck is queued up. The last thing you want is to discover that the person you emailed it through to is off sick and no one knows where it ended up. Even if you can sort it out in the nick of time, it will throw you off course before you've even begun.

You might be a bit nervous before you start, so spend a couple of minutes slowly breathing in through your nose and out through your mouth. It doesn't sound like it would do anything, but it really will help calm your nerves.

It's important to get off to a good start. I've already said you need to know what you're going to say, and this is doubly true for your intro. You don't want to stumble over your words here as it will blow your confidence for the rest of the presentation. So learn it by rote and deliver it confidently. This will relax you and grab the audience.

Decide beforehand whether you mind people interrupting with questions or if you'd rather they wait until the end. The latter is obviously easiest as you won't get thrown off track, but if you feel confident fielding questions mid-flow, you'll look like a real pro. Set this out as part of your introduction.

If you do make a mistake, just laugh it off (even if you're dying inside) and start that bit again.

Project your voice and be animated and enthusiastic. Enthusiasm's infectious: you'll notice the audience responding positively. Don't be afraid to be a bit emotive too.

You do want questions at the end because a) you want people to know more about your project, and b) it'll really fall flat if no one has any. So don't just ask limply if anyone has questions. Get on the front foot: 'I'm sure there are a lot of questions. Who'd like to go first?' I promise you this works. You might well get someone with an axe to grind who'll try and trip you up with a hand-grenade question. Deal with it as best you can and don't be afraid to push back a bit. Use it to try and get a bit of a discussion going: 'What does everyone else think?'

So with a lot of preparation and plenty of practice this is a skill you can definitely master, and you'll be able to offer something a bit better than all the average presentations you've sat through. Who knows, maybe you'll eventually learn to enjoy it.

Things go wrong – that's inevitable. No matter how on top of your risks and issues you are, or how great your planning assumptions were, or how on the ball your team is, at some point things will go badly wrong. It may be due to something you or your team did, or failed to foresee, or it may be due to some external factor that was completely beyond your control. In either case, how you respond is likely to have a bearing on the impact of the problem.

The most important thing is to put the problem in context. At some point a supplier won't deliver to time, an internal team will let you down, a key person will suddenly leave. Yes, these are problems, and they'll probably delay your project timeline. But they aren't the end of the world. If you treat them as though they are, you're in danger of making a drama out of a crisis, and that can be contagious within the team. Before you know it, you've talked yourself into a disaster. How does this look to your management? It looks like you aren't coping with an issue that has affected every single project since projects began. The key is not to take it personally and to immediately start working out what you're going to do about it.

How long is this delay likely to be? What are the cost implications? Are these within the project's tolerances? If not, can we descope elements of the project and deliver them later? Hopefully, you can come up with a few options, which you can discuss with your team and then take to your management. The key point is that you're reacting quickly to the situation and not waiting for direction on what to do next.

It's important not to discuss your options externally at this point, particularly where suppliers are involved. Your management or sponsors might want to take a different course of action and they'll certainly need to approve whatever ends up being the plan going forward. If you've already entered into external conversations about options, and set supplier expectations, you risk undermining yourself further down the line.

So react quickly, but don't share your thinking externally and, most importantly, don't take it personally.

But what if it really was your fault? We're all fallible and we all make mistakes. Don't ever try and cover it up or point the finger elsewhere. Own up to it quickly, explain how it happened and, again, immediately plan your way out of it. Too much publicly beating yourself up isn't a good look and it won't help the situation. If someone on your team has messed up, then it's still on you to take responsibility; you were happy enough to take the plaudits when things were going well ...

The real doomsday scenario is that your project gets pulled – and this will happen to you at some point. If it does, then it's incumbent on you to ensure things are shut down properly: that the documentation is up to date and the budgets tied up, etc. The most difficult part of this is that these things rarely happen out of the blue. You and your team may well have been working under the shadow of this threat for some time. This is where you really do need to demonstrate leadership. The last thing you want is for everyone to down tools and start drifting off. So stay positive, and encourage the team to focus on what they can control and not be distracted by what they can't. Whatever happens, you'll get points for professionalism.

Whatever the setback, it's important to learn from it and to be honest with yourself about what actually went wrong, and how it maybe could have been avoided. What would you do differently next time? Did you put too much faith in that supplier? Did you ignore that problem because it was easier than having a difficult conversation? Most of the content of this book has been informed by things going wrong so you're in good company.

But perhaps the most important lesson on things going wrong is not to be consumed by a fear of it. That just leads to indecision and inertia which is a guaranteed route to failure.

Hopefully you'll have noticed a few common themes running through these chapters. The most important one to understand is that it's your responsibility to provide leadership, with all that entails, to the project. It's up to you to set a behavioural example. It's up to you to reach out to the stakeholders and manage the suppliers, to make sure the plans are up to date, that the board runs well, that the budgets balance, that decisions are being made, and that the deliverables are being delivered.

Of course, you don't have to personally do all these things, but you do have to take responsibility for them. So you need to be clear about what you expect from people: the team, stakeholders, suppliers and management. Miscommunication can be the root of so many problems. Make sure you're explaining things clearly, whether that's your expectations for a task, your position on a situation, your board papers – whatever. And don't be afraid to check other people's understanding. People often hear what they want to hear, not what you've actually said.

You do need to give yourself time to do things properly. Forget multi-tasking; it's a myth. If you're in a meeting and reading your emails at the same time, you aren't properly concentrating on the meeting and you aren't really taking in your emails either. Also, it's rude. So block out time. The number one cause of stress is having to complete tasks in too little time.

If you're constantly finding yourself under pressure, that's probably a sign you could be utilising your team more. Do you really need to be at every supplier workshop? Could someone else not lead on some of them? Providing leadership doesn't mean you have to be omnipresent. Remember you want to empower your team; you won't do that by making everything about you. Also, people want to be challenged and stretched. I've known far more people leave projects because they didn't feel they were gaining enough experience than because they felt overwhelmed.

Don't be afraid to ask for help, whether that's from your team, your manager, or anyone in your network. Another major cause of stress is internalising problems and trying to solve everything yourself. No one expects you to be able to do that. There'll be a huge amount of experience across the people you're dealing with, so tap into it. Even just getting another perspective can really help.

Be proactive. It's really easy to become blown around by events; the more you can get ahead of them the better. So don't ignore those flashing warning lights from that supplier who's just suddenly gone cold on you, or that internal team who seem to be going off in a different direction. It means putting your head above the parapet and challenging – although obviously you need to do this in a collegial, positive way. But never duck these inevitably difficult conversations. The sooner you have them the better.

Don't mistake good housekeeping for good project management. This is a common pitfall. Yes, all the documentation needs to be up to date and the board papers need to go out on time, and yes, it will reflect badly on you if these things aren't happening. But you're a PM, not a PMO. The risk and issues log being up to date isn't the same thing as the risks and issues being managed well.

Prioritise talking to your stakeholders. An hour chatting to a potentially influential stakeholder isn't an hour when you really should have been doing something seemingly more tangible like reviewing your plans. It's an important task in itself. You must keep yourself and your project in people's sight. You're part sales rep in this regard.

Actually, you need to keep talking to everyone: your team, your suppliers, your boss … everybody. But make sure you're listening as well as talking. Whatever the situation, try and put yourself in other people's shoes. Why are they taking this position? Why have they done a 180-degree turn since the last time you spoke (which was only yesterday)? It's probably not just to wind you up. In their place, might you actually be saying the same thing? What's changed from their viewpoint? Have you contributed to this? (Be honest.) This doesn't mean you have to agree or accept their position, but it's a good skill to be able to step back and understand what's driving someone else's stance. You can then engage better to try and get them round to your way of thinking.

Make sure you're dealing in facts. People can often present their opinion as fact or exaggerate things. This is particularly true when things are going awry. It's your job to step back, take wider soundings and come to a view on exactly what the situation is and what can be done to rectify it. Don't get dragged into melodrama and other people's agendas.

It's worth stressing that staying the course on a project will give you far more meaningful experience than flitting around from project to project. A lot of people do move around a lot to raise their profile and chase promotions. This can work, especially in the short term, but you'll never really immerse yourself in the project lifecycle and your part in it. You'll be a much better prospect for a promotion if you've stuck in there through the ups and downs, and it actually does look better on your CV.

Lastly, and I think this is overlooked with most jobs, you really should try and enjoy it. You've created a motivated team with a shared sense of purpose. You've built a good relationship with your suppliers and other stakeholders, who trust you even when they don't agree with you. And your senior management have complete faith in you. What's not to like? Of course, not every day's going to be completely optimal, but there will come a point when you've finally gone live. Ok, it may be a bit later than you'd initially planned, and it might fall slightly short of your original shiny vision. But it's gone live – and a massive part of that's on you.

About the author

Jon Calpin has worked in the IT industry in both the public and private sectors for over 25 years, initially working in technical roles before moving into project and programme management.

He has spent the last 15 years working as a programme manager in digital health. During this time, he's led on the national implementation of the Summary Care Record, the procurement and migration of NHSMail2, and the roll-out of the clinical terminology SNOMED to the primary care estate in England. He is now a consultant, most recently working in the genomics sector.

Printed in Great Britain
by Amazon